# HELP!
## For Primary Art

by Belva Lightner Hough

Fearon Teacher Aids
a division of
**David S. Lake Publishers**
Belmont, California

*Publisher:* Mel Cebulash
*Editorial director:* Ina Tabibian
*Editor:* Diane Whitworth
*Managing editor:* Susan J. Riddle
*Production editor:* Stephen Feinstein
*Design director:* Eleanor Mennick
*Designer:* Colleen Forbes
*Cover designer:* Colleen Forbes
*Illustrator:* Duane Bibby
*Manufacturing director:* Casimira Kostecki

Entire contents copyright © 1986 by David S. Lake Publishers, 19 Davis Drive, Belmont, CA 94002. All rights reserved. No part of this book may be reproduced by any means, transmitted, or translated into a machine language, without written permission from the publisher.

ISBN-0-8224-3615-9

Library of Congress Catalog Card Number: 84-052853

Printed in the United States of America

1. 9 8 7 6 5 4 3

*This book is dedicated to my second-grade colleagues, past and present, at A. M. Pate Elementary School who have taught me so much.*

*And especially, this little volume is dedicated to Robin, Steve, Maureen, and Lee for their sustaining belief that Mom could do it.*

# Table of Contents

Introduction .................................................. vi
A Few Tips about Art Instruction ........................ vii

### I. A Piece of Manila, A Box of Crayons
Word Fun ..................................................... 2
Stained-Glass Pictures .................................... 3
Repeat the Design ......................................... 5
Shoe Show Time ............................................ 7
Color Walk .................................................. 9
Giraff-a-gators and Bunn-a-flies ........................ 10
The Eyes Have It .......................................... 12
Loooooooong Pictures .................................... 14

### II. Paper, Crayons, Scissors, and Paste
Twirling Figures ........................................... 16
Hound Dog .................................................. 19
Halloween Poppers ........................................ 22
Hand Spring ................................................ 25
Rabbit Puppets ............................................ 28
Mosaic Designs ............................................ 30
Fish 'n' Fun ................................................ 32
Spring-a-lings ............................................. 34

### III. The Basics Plus One or Two
Teddy Bears on Parade ................................... 38
Tree Seasons .............................................. 41
Christmas Wreaths ........................................ 43
Autograph Mirrors ........................................ 45
Magnetic Magic ............................................ 48
Sun Catchers .............................................. 50
Ghosts! ..................................................... 52
Leaf Rubbings ............................................. 53

# Introduction

Hello, dear primary teacher—you who are trying to give some special help to Mary in her reading, *and* get your attendance report finished for the office, *and* respond to Johnny's mother about his lost lunch money, *and* present an enjoyable as well as successful art lesson—be of good cheer. *HELP!* is here.

Open this book to any art lesson in the first two sections, and your ready-to-use lesson is before you. Only the ideas in Section III require special materials or preparation and need to be read the day before you plan to teach the lesson.

Some of these ideas may have been used on the ark. They are old but loved, and new to each generation. Perhaps you will see ideas here that you have used in the past but have forgotten. Like old friends, these art activities are always welcome. You will be glad to see them again. Also, there are many new ideas here for you and your children to enjoy. Whether the art lessons are old or new, they have been tested with primary children for ease of use and appropriateness.

*HELP! For Primary Art* is divided into three sections.

- Section I: *A Piece of Manila, a Box of Crayons* provides lessons that require only these two materials—and your enthusiastic motivation.
- Section II: *Paper, Crayons, Scissors, and Paste* offers simple, child-pleasing projects that use readily available materials.
- Section III: *The Basics Plus One or Two* demonstrates delightful lessons that require a minimum of preparation and "outside" materials.

# A Few Tips about Art Instruction

Most primary schoolchildren are eager to please their teachers. In math, reading, and other academic subjects where there are right ways and wrong ways to do things, children gain approval by doing things the right way. Eager to please, the children also look for the right way to do art work. It may be necessary for you, the teacher, to stress again and again that in art there is no *right* way or *wrong* way; there is just your *best* way. Rigidity in art lessons can be deadly. Encourage imagination and spontaneity.

**Techniques to encourage children's art**
All of the above is not to imply that the teacher should say nothing and simply pass out paper and crayons or paint. That will not make a successful art lesson.

One of the first things I tell my students is, "I am not a very good artist, and I know your trees (or whatever) will be much better than mine." Then I ask them to think about trees, and we discuss what we see when we look at a tree. One child will mention the trunk, another the branches, still another will tell about leaves or seed pods. As the children call out these things, I draw a very rudimentary tree on the chalkboard that attempts to picture their observations about trees. As the tree is finished, I ask the children, "Does your tree have to look like Mrs. Hough's tree?" They all know the answer, "Certainly not!"

If you are lucky enough to have a tree growing outside your windows, use it as inspiration, or take the class on a walk to look at trees. You can ask your children to pretend to draw in the air, using their index fingers as crayons.

Most of us go through the world looking but not really seeing. Art can be a means of heightening a child's awareness of the environment. For instance, if you plan to draw trees, on the day before the lesson ask your children to look closely at trees—for homework. Tell each child to choose a tree and feel it, listen to it, smell it, look at it up close, and then stand back to look at the whole tree at once. Children can also ask their parents the names of trees. You can then lead a class discussion about trees before crayon is ever put to paper. Your little artists need to be inspired!

Have your children draw only, only, only with crayons! Their muscles are not developed enough for the intricacies of tiny pencil drawings, and the uninhibited expressions of early childhood can be so easily lost.

Encourage your artists to draw one thing on a page. If they are drawing owls, then ask them to draw just one big owl—no sky, no grass—just owl.

Children will be more pleased with their efforts (and that's the bottom line) if their colors are vivid, so for most art work, encourage your artists to make their colors "dark, dark, and shiny bright."

Try this simple technique to help children get their drawings on paper without frustration. Draw a facsimile of a sheet of paper on the chalkboard. Then discuss drawing a cat (or other subject). Ask, "Would you put the cat's head here at the bottom of the page? Why not?" You can also use the human figure as an example. Have the children stand and pretend they are leaning against a giant piece of paper. Ask them to imagine, "Where would your feet be on this giant piece of paper? What about your waist? Your head? Where would your knees be on the paper?"

Of course there is more to the primary art program than drawing. Other learning experiences include folding paper, cutting (the skill of using scissors is very important for little fingers), and pasting. There is even learning to use patterns, although these should be used on a very limited basis. There is also the joy of taking one thing and turning it into something else—cutting shapes out of fine sandpaper, pasting popcorn onto paper to form designs. Art is never a mimeographed picture to color.

Many primary grades use tempera and finger paints, especially where there is an art room. In other schools, where primary art is taught in the regular classroom, the realities of life have to be faced: if there is carpeting on the floor, the painting experiences are going to be very limited.

**Techniques for keeping the art lesson under control**

The art session is a more relaxed time of the day. During the art lesson, there can be a free atmosphere with more chatting and moving about. There is definitely a very fine line between creative atmosphere and chaos. A chaotic environment does not contribute to creativity in the long run. Insist that while directions for and discussions about art projects are going on, all students pay careful attention. Children should not have crayons in their hands during this time. When inspiration and instruction time are over, then say, "Let's begin now." The whole group goes to work immediately.

A child who has derived no particular satisfaction or success from past art experiences may very quickly draw an owl in a careless, thoughtless manner and say, "I'm through. What can I do now?" Or this child may scribble carelessly on both sides of the paper and announce, "I messed up."

You may be able to avoid such problems if you make it clear from the beginning of the lesson that the material you are about to present will be the complete art lesson for the day. You could say, "Take your time and do a nice job. When you are finished with your project, you may read in your supplementary reader. After everyone is finished, we will have an art show." This may help to head off the child who feels it is the teacher's job to entertain with a new "trick" every minute of the day or the child who sees an art lesson as an opportunity to entertain the class.

Children should understand that there is not an endless supply of art paper available. They may not thoughtlessly waste paper and say, "I messed up." ("Therefore, I don't have to try this," may be the real message here.) If possible, put the child who says this back on track by showing how some of the lines can be incorporated into a more satisfactory drawing, or how to fold the paper to have space for another try. Of course, there are times when another sheet of paper will be necessary, but children should not be encouraged to expect it.

### Ways to share art work

Art work is meant to be shared, but plan ahead for sharing or every child will want to show you the project-in-progress three or four times. Then the first thing you know, things are out of hand. Make sure the students know that they can expect to share their art projects at the end of the lesson. Here are some suggestions:

- Let the children show their work to the class, row by row or group by group, at the end of the art lesson.

- Arrange with the teacher next door for your class to go over and share the art projects.

- Send art projects home with the students.

- Ask the class to number off. Then call out pairs of numbers and allow students to share art projects with their number partners. Set a kitchen timer for five minutes or so and tell the students, "I'll set the timer and when the bell rings, we'll all go back to our seats."

- Have the children bring art projects to you as they are finished, and help them pin the projects on the class bulletin board. You can also display art in the hall.

- Encourage your students and enjoy art lessons with them. Share your enthusiasm for their efforts, and your students will respond positively.

# I  A Piece of Manila, A Box of Crayons

# Word Fun

## Objective:
Students will express the meanings of words through art.

## Materials
9″ × 12″ manila paper
crayons

## Demonstration/Motivation
Ask students to call out some describing words for you to write on the chalkboard. You should include some words of your own. Demonstrate the word *fat*.

Ask a volunteer to come to the chalkboard and draw one of the words listed. Then ask the students how they would draw *cold* and *polka dot*.

## Procedures
Pass out manila paper and crayons. Ask the children to choose words from the chalkboard or use other words to create word drawings. Tell them they may draw words in any direction—slanted, upside down, and straight across. Offer to help with the spelling of special words that students may know how to pronounce but not how to spell.

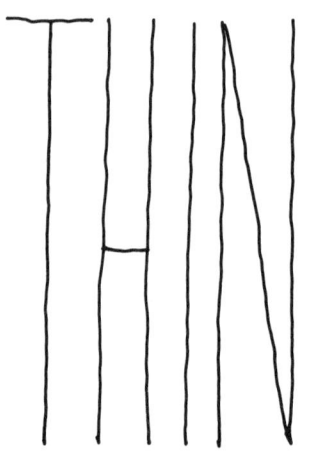

# Stained-Glass Pictures

## Objective:
Students will make crayon outline drawings that illustrate the concept of contrast.

## Materials

9" × 12" manila paper

crayons

## Demonstration/Motivation

Draw and color two solid red squares on a piece of paper. Outline one square in heavy black crayon. Hold the squares up and ask the students which one shows up the best (the one outlined in black will). Talk about contrast.

## Procedures

Pass out paper and crayons. Tell the students they are going to make crayon drawings that use contrast for emphasis.

### STEP 1

Direct the students to draw simple scenes with a few large objects, such as trees, animals, butterflies, the sun. Tell them to press hard on their crayons so that the colors in their pictures will be shiny.

**STEP 2**

Now have the students outline some areas of their drawings with black crayon. This process will highlight these areas and emphasize their positions in the students' pictures. Lead them to see that this is only one way to draw.

# Repeat the Design

## Objective:
Students will create designs and draw them repeatedly on pieces of folded paper. The finished overall designs may be used for wrapping paper, place mats, or book covers. These designs may have a seasonal theme, such as pumpkins, Christmas trees, hearts, or turkeys.

## Materials

9" × 12" manila or colored construction paper

crayons

## Demonstration/Motivation

Tell the students they are going to make designs. Have each child think of a simple figure (such as a flower) to draw many times to create an overall design. Draw a flower (or other simple figure) on the chalkboard. Help the children think of other simple figures (a ship, a candle, a heart, a butterfly, a kite, or a pumpkin). Illustrate a few on the chalkboard, or have the students come to the board and draw their ideas.

## Procedures

Pass out paper and crayons. Tell the students you are going to show them how to fold the paper, so they must listen carefully to your directions. Demonstrate each step for the students, then repeat the step along with them. Walk around the room checking on their progress, to be sure your directions are being followed.

**STEP**

"Fold the paper in half, keep it folded, and always folding the short sides together, fold it in half three more times (four times altogether). Be sure your edges meet, and press down hard along your folds each time."

**STEP**

"Open the paper. Notice that it is now divided into four rows of four frames each." Draw a facsimile on the chalkboard, using dotted lines to represent fold lines.

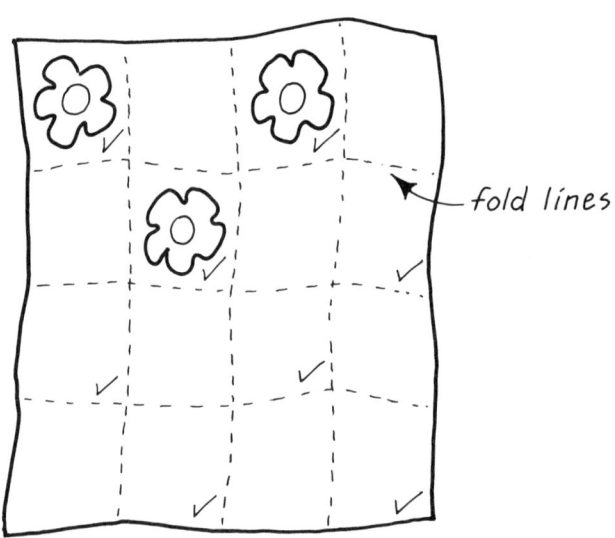

**STEP**

"We're now going to draw our designs on our papers. On row one, put the design in squares one and three; row two, in squares two and four; row three, in squares one and three. I'll put a check in each box where you will draw, but once you get started you will see that it is easy because your design will be drawn in every other box. You will repeat your drawing eight times. Make them as nearly alike as you possibly can."

**STEP**

If they wish, older children may trace over the fold lines with a sharp crayon, using a ruler for a guide. When the designs are finished, discuss with the children uses for repeated designs—wrapping paper, fabrics, patchwork quilts, and place mats.

# Shoe Show Time

## Objective:
Students will draw figures using the outlines of their shoes.

## Materials
9″ × 12″ manila paper

crayons

shoe

## Demonstration/Motivation

Tell the students they are going to use their shoes for this activity. Take off one of your shoes or borrow one from a student. Hold the shoe vertically against the chalkboard and draw around it. Taking the shoe away, ask the students what they see. Could it be a rabbit? Finish the drawing so that it looks like a rabbit or another figure.

Now hold the shoe horizontally against the chalkboard and draw around it again. What do the students think it could be? Have a volunteer come to the chalkboard to finish the drawing. Have the other students make suggestions.

# Procedures

Pass out paper and crayons. Have each student place a shoe on the paper and outline it with a crayon. Then challenge them to create something new from their shoe outlines. Tell the students to make their drawings different from what has already been drawn on the chalkboard. The students may place their shoes in any direction on the paper—slanted, upside down, or straight across. When all creations are finished, have a "Shoe Show" and let the students show their favorite drawings.

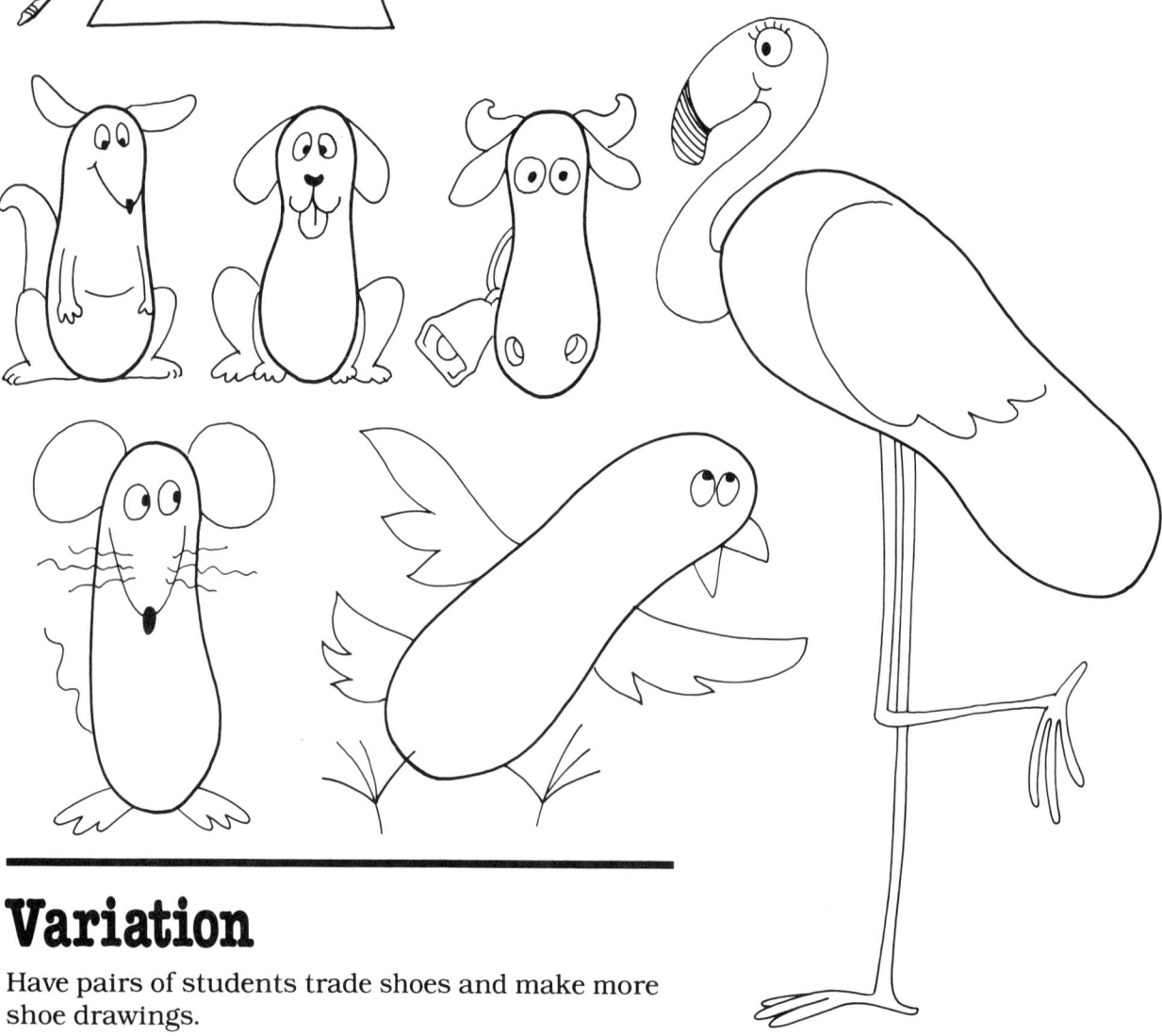

# Variation

Have pairs of students trade shoes and make more shoe drawings.

# Color Walk

**Objective:** Students will become more aware of their environment by taking a class walk, looking for objects of a designated color, and then drawing pictures of what they find.

## Materials

9" × 12" manila paper

crayons

## Demonstration/Motivation

Tell the students to look around the classroom and call out the different colors they see. Encourage them to look carefully so they can see even the smallest colored objects.

## Procedures

Have each student choose a color or have the whole class choose one color. Then go on a class walk, inside or outside. Instruct the students to look for things that are the chosen color. When you return to the classroom, pass out paper and crayons. Tell the students to draw all they saw that was the designated color. Older students can label their objects, too. Somctimes it is fun to have a contest and see who can find the most!

## Variation

Have each student choose a color, think about it, and make observations as a homework assignment. For example, the students can look for green, red, or blue things and make their drawings the next day in class. Some children may like the challenge of looking for less frequently seen colors, like orange or purple.

# Giraff-a-gators and Bunn-a-flies

## Objective:
Students will draw and name new creatures by combining body parts of two real animals.

## Materials
9" × 12" manila paper

crayons

## Demonstration/Motivation
Draw on the chalkboard an imaginary animal that is made of the body parts of two real animals, like a giraffe and an alligator.

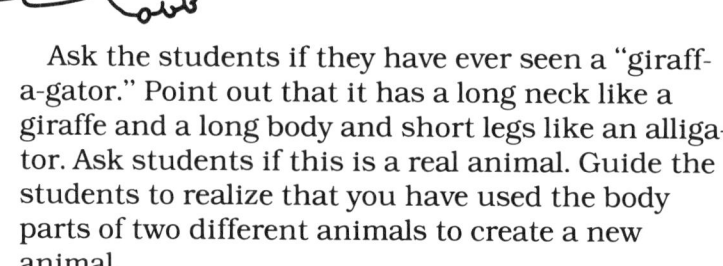

Ask the students if they have ever seen a "giraff-a-gator." Point out that it has a long neck like a giraffe and a long body and short legs like an alligator. Ask students if this is a real animal. Guide the students to realize that you have used the body parts of two different animals to create a new animal.

Ask the students to tell you what they think a "bunn-a-fly" looks like. What two real animals could make up a bunn-a-fly? Two suggestions from the students might be a bunny rabbit and a butterfly. Have a volunteer come to the chalkboard and draw part of a bunn-a-fly. Then choose another student to finish the drawing.

# Procedures

Pass out manila paper and crayons. As you do this, help the students name as many animals as they can. Now challenge them to draw imaginary animals that combine the body parts of two real animals. Tell them to give their animals names when they are finished drawing. After the students have completed their creations, let them show their animals and tell what they have named them.

# Variation

The more advanced students may wish to use body parts from more than two animals to create their creatures. They can also write stories about their animals, telling where they live, what they eat, the sounds they make, and any other facts they wish to include.

# The Eyes Have It

**Objective:** After marking eight pairs of dots on their papers, students will draw faces, using these dots as the eyes.

## Materials

9″ × 12″ manila paper

crayons

## Demonstration/Motivation

Draw a facsimile of the art paper on the chalkboard. On the paper draw eight pairs of dots. Ask the students what they think you have drawn. Usually someone will guess that the dots could be eyes. You may need to help a little by pointing to your own eyes or giving other hints. Then ask *whose* eyes they are. Lead the students to see that these eyes could belong to people, animals, trolls, elves, dragons, ghosts, and the like. Ask a few volunteers to come to the chalkboard and draw faces around the eyes.

# Procedures

Pass out paper and crayons to the students. Ask them to draw eight pairs of dots on their papers, just as you have done on the chalkboard. Tell them to scatter them about and to make each pair a different color. Direct the students to draw faces that they imagine will go with the eyes they have drawn. Stress that they are to draw only faces. With younger students you may need to discuss facial parts and expressions. When students are finished, let them exchange papers and look at, discuss, and enjoy each other's creations.

# Variation

Have each student create a face around a pair of "big" eyes. The students can draw the eyes themselves, or you can do it for them. If you decide to do it for them, have the students pass by your desk with their papers, and quickly draw the big eyes with a black marker.

# Looooooong Pictures

**Objective:** Students will draw things that are long on narrow strips of paper.

## Materials

9″ × 12″ manila paper cut into 3″ × 12″ strips

crayons

## Demonstration/Motivation

Ask the students to give examples of things that are long. You will get replies such as snake, train, and rocket. Some clever child will see the possibility of turning the paper vertically and will suggest a waterfall.

## Procedures

Pass out paper and crayons. Direct the students to draw long pictures. Tell them they may draw anything, but they must use the entire length of their papers. As the students finish, show your delight and pleasure with their work. Do lots of praising and give many, many positive comments as you display their pictures on the bulletin board.

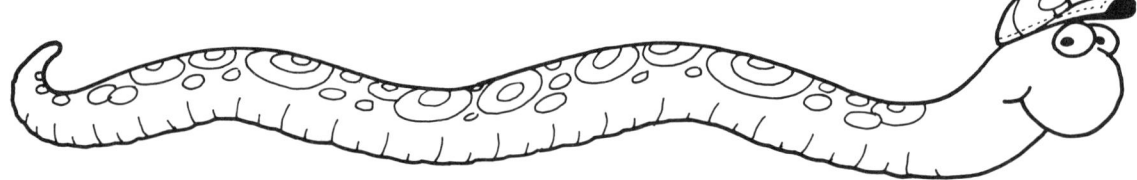

# II Paper, Crayons, Scissors, and Paste

# Twirling Figures

**Objective:** Using a basic folding procedure, students will create individual figures. They will follow verbal directions and illustrations carefully. These figures may take a seasonal theme, such as jack-o'-lanterns, snowmen, spring bunnies, or Santa shapes.

## Materials

- 9″ × 12″ manila or bond paper
- scissors
- paste
- crayons
- hole punch or pencil
- string or yarn
- rubber bands (optional)

## Procedures

Pass out paper, crayons, paste, and scissors to the students. Tell the students they are going to make twirling figures, and they must listen to your directions carefully. Demonstrate each step for the children, then repeat the step along with them. Spot check on their progress to avoid big problems later.

### STEP

"Fold the paper in half, keep it folded, and always folding the longer edges together, fold it in half two more times (three times altogether)."

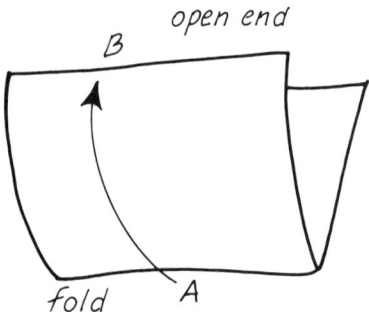 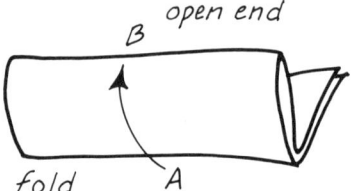 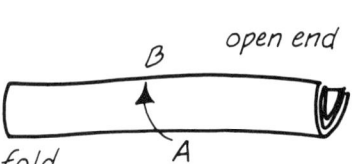

**STEP**

"Open the paper. We will use the fold lines as guides." Place your own paper on the chalkboard and demonstrate this step for the children. "Fold forward on the first crease. Then turn the folded side face down on your desks and fold forward on the next crease. Continue folding until all creases have been folded." (This is, of course, a basic fanfold.)

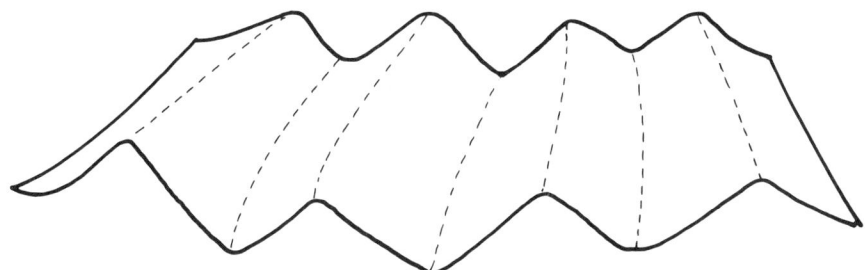

**STEP**

"We're going to draw half a figure on one outside fold of the paper." Show students how to draw a figure on the paper. A snowman, an astronaut, or a fantasy figure may work well. "After you have drawn the shapes, cut along the lines. Be sure not to cut on the fold."

*open end*   *fold*

**STEP**

"Unfold the figures carefully. Color in details with your crayons."

**STEP**

"Turn the colored figures face down on your desks. Refold on each crease in the opposite direction." Demonstrate this step for the children. Say, "Put letters on your figures in this order," while you draw the diagram below on the chalkboard to illustrate the order of letters.

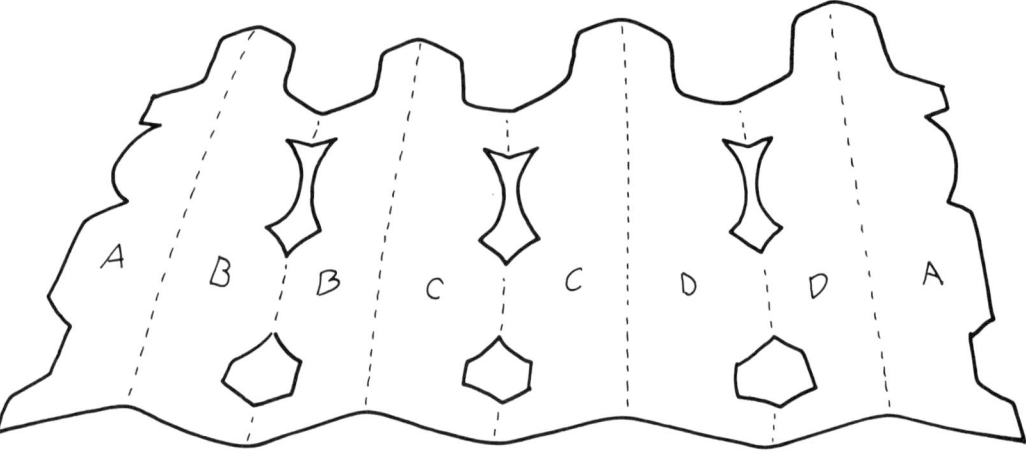

**STEP**

"Paste the *B*'s together, paste the *C*'s together, the *D*'s, and finally the *A*'s." Be sure to check the students' lettering and folding before they start pasting.

**STEP**

Make a hole in the top of each figure with a hole punch or pencil. Insert a string or some yarn into the holes and hang the figures from light fixtures, from hooks in the ceiling, or in a window. Long rubber bands, in place of string, may be wound up and let go to create action figures.

# Hound Dog

## Objective:
Using a basic folding procedure, students will make hound dog bookmarks. They will add facial features by cutting and pasting.

## Materials

brown 9″ × 12″ construction paper cut into 9″ × 6″ pieces

small pieces of red, white, and black construction paper

scissors

paste

crayons

## Demonstration/Motivation

Show the students a finished hound dog bookmark. Ask them what features on the dog's face reveal that it is a hound dog. Students will probably say its long ears and big eyes.

## Procedures

Pass out paper, scissors, crayons, and paste. Tell the students they are going to make hound dog bookmarks. They must watch and listen carefully as you demonstrate each step. As you demonstrate, try to move around the room to check the students' progress.

### STEP

"First we are going to make a square. Put the piece of brown paper in front of you (vertically). Fold the right bottom corner up to the left side, until the edges meet. Press down hard along the fold to crease it well."

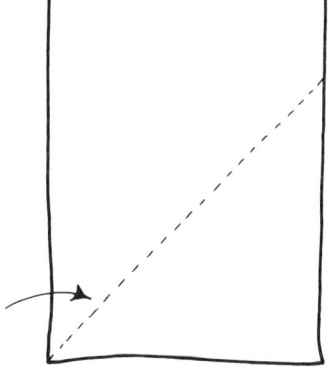

19

**STEP**

"Carefully cut off the excess piece at the top and put it aside. We will use it later."

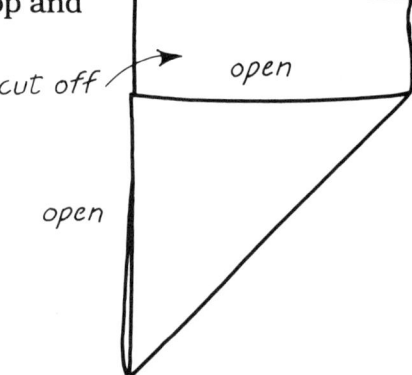

**STEP**

"Keeping the paper folded, place it in front of you, flat on your desk, so the center point of the triangle is pointing straight at you. With a crayon you will mark where the eyes and nose will be pasted. First put a little circle at the center point of the triangle. This will be where you paste the nose. Then make two small circles close together in the middle of the triangle, centered above the nose. These will be the eyes." As you talk, demonstrate the series of steps for your students.

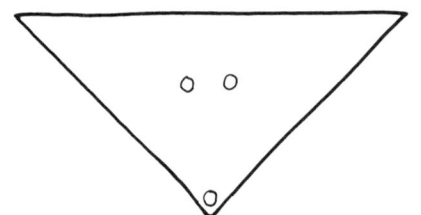

**STEP**

Show the students how to cut the eyes, nose, mouth, and tongue from the pieces of construction paper they have. Suggest they fold the paper so that they can cut two eyes at the same time. "Using the white paper first, fold it in half and draw a big eye with your crayon. Cut out and paste the eyes on your dog's face. Then fold your black paper in half and draw a smaller circle for the inner eyes. Cut them out and paste them on top of the white circles. Cut out a round black nose and paste it on the dog's face. Make a tongue from the red paper and paste it inside the mouth (open edge of triangle at the point under the nose)."

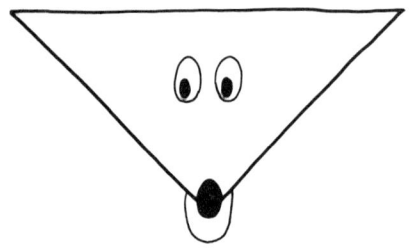

**STEP**

"We will now make the ears of our hound dog. First fold the right corner of the triangle down toward the center point until the tip of the corner overlaps the right open edge of the triangle and the top closed edge just touches the right eye. Press hard along the crease. Then do the same with the left corner. Fold it down toward the center point until it overlaps the left open edge and the top closed edge barely touches the left eye. Crease the fold crisply." Demonstrate these steps carefully and help those students experiencing difficulty.

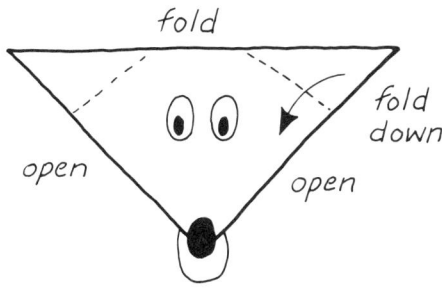

**STEP**

"Now find the remaining piece of brown paper I asked you to put aside. Fold it in half the long way and paste the edges together. When this is done, paste it to the back of your dog. You now have a bookmark."

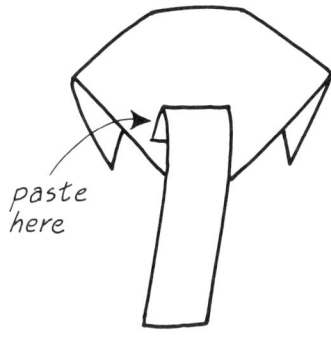

# Variation

You may wish to have your students make puppets. Take the piece of folded brown paper (see Step 6) and fold up the end one inch. Paste the folded end to the center of the back of the dog. This creates a handle for the puppet.

Teach the students the song, "How Much Is That Doggie in the Window?" If you are in a one-story building, arrange with the teacher next door for a surprise visit. Ask him or her to open the classroom windows. Have your class slip quietly under the windows, put just their puppets' heads through the windows, and sing a few choruses of "How Much Is That Doggie in the Window?"

# Halloween Poppers

**Objective:** Using paste and colored paper, students will achieve 3-D effects on their crayon drawings. This project is adaptable to any holiday.

## Materials

9″ × 12″ black construction paper

small pieces of colored construction paper

4″ × ¼″ strips of black construction paper (six for each student)

crayons

scissors

paste

## Demonstration/Motivation

Ask the students what the symbols of Halloween are (pumpkins, bats, ghosts, the moon, witches, cats, a haunted house, a graveyard). Show a sample of a Halloween popper picture you have already made. Tell the students they are going to make their own popper pictures.

## Procedures

Pass out black paper and scissors. If this project is to be completed in one day, set out pieces of colored construction paper, too.

### STEP 1

"Children, first I want you to plan your pictures. Remember, this is a Halloween (Christmas, Thanksgiving . . . ) night scene. The black paper represents the sky, and you will need to make a line to represent the ground. Perhaps you want to add a fence. Everything you draw on your papers must be colored very, very firmly and heavily so that it will stand out. Some colors that show up very well are brown, green, orange, white, yellow, red, and purple. As you draw, think about three objects you will paste on your scene. Perhaps one

22

will be a black cat sitting on a fence. Another might be a bright, full moon in the sky. Let me see your pictures when you are finished coloring." Students may rush through this part to get to the poppers. If you want spectacular pictures, don't allow them to hurry at this stage. Be sure students press down hard on their crayons and make their colors really shiny.

## STEP

When most students have finished coloring their scenes (or the next day), let them begin drawing and cutting out the three objects they will add to their scenes. Talk about proportion. Draw a simple scene on the chalkboard. Then say, "I want to cut out a pumpkin for my picture." Draw a pumpkin that is much too large and ask the students what is wrong with it. Then draw another pumpkin that is too small and discuss its size in relation to the drawing. Lead the children to understand that the objects they will now cut out of colored paper must be in proportion to the scene they have drawn. "You may now come up to the table and choose the colors you will need to make the three objects that will pop up from your pictures."

## STEP

Now the students are ready to make the poppers and paste them to their pictures. Provide each student with six strips of black paper, approximately 4" × ¼". Demonstrate with larger strips how to fold them correctly. "First put paste on the tip of strip B, then attach strip B to the tip of strip A." Walk around the room at this point and help those who need it.

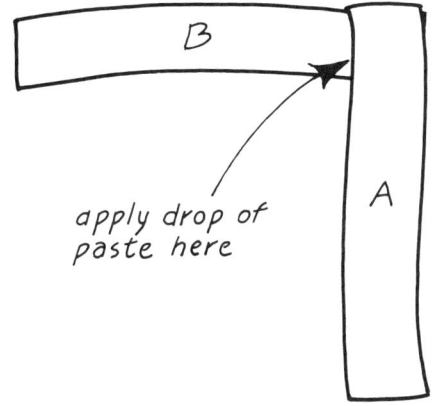

**STEP**

Draw the diagram from Step 3 on the chalkboard, labeling strip *A* and strip *B*. This will aid in explaining the folding procedure. Place your two strips on the chalkboard, next to the diagram, and demonstrate this step. "Fold strip *B* to the right, over strip *A*. Then fold strip *A* up and over *B*. Fold strip *B* back to the left, over *A*. Fold strip *A* back down to its original position. Start again, folding strip *B* over *A* to the right, strip *A* up and over *B*, then strip *B* back to the left, and *A* down to the first position. Repeat this procedure—fold over, up, back, and down until you have a finished popper. Make two more poppers in the same way. I will be around to assist you if you need it." If this comes easily to some students, ask them to be your helpers and aid others who are having difficulty.

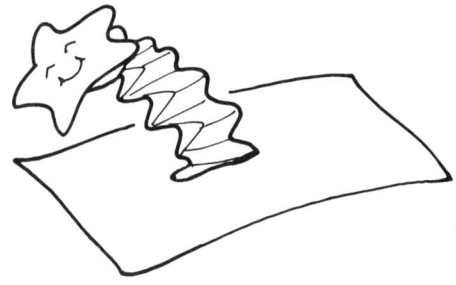

**STEP**

"We are now ready to paste the poppers on our pictures. The best way is to put a dot of paste where you want the popper to be on your picture and stick the popper to it. Then put a little dab of paste on the top of the popper and put your object on top. Press it down until the paste holds." Demonstrate on the chalkboard picture with a cut-out pumpkin. Remind the students to use the paste sparingly—a little goes a long way. As you circulate, hold up examples of good work for everyone to see. The children will quickly get the idea.

**STEP**

Choose several students to help you put these pictures on the bulletin board in the room or the hall. They will make an outstanding seasonal display.

# Hand Spring

## Objective:
Students will create flowers by drawing around their hands.

## Materials

12" × 18" colored construction paper

crayons

scissors

paste

## Demonstration/Motivation

Tell the students they will be using their hands as patterns to make spring flowers. Demonstrate how this is done. Hold your hand against the chalkboard, keeping your fingers together and the thumb tucked in against the palm. Draw around your hand, along the outside of the fingers and not between them. Close up the shape so it resembles a flower. Then add a stem and leaves to finish the drawing. You may wish to demonstrate how to draw two leaf styles. Two drawing strokes are used: a rainbow (⌒) and a rocker (⌣). Say each stroke (rainbow or rocker) as you use it to draw the leaves.

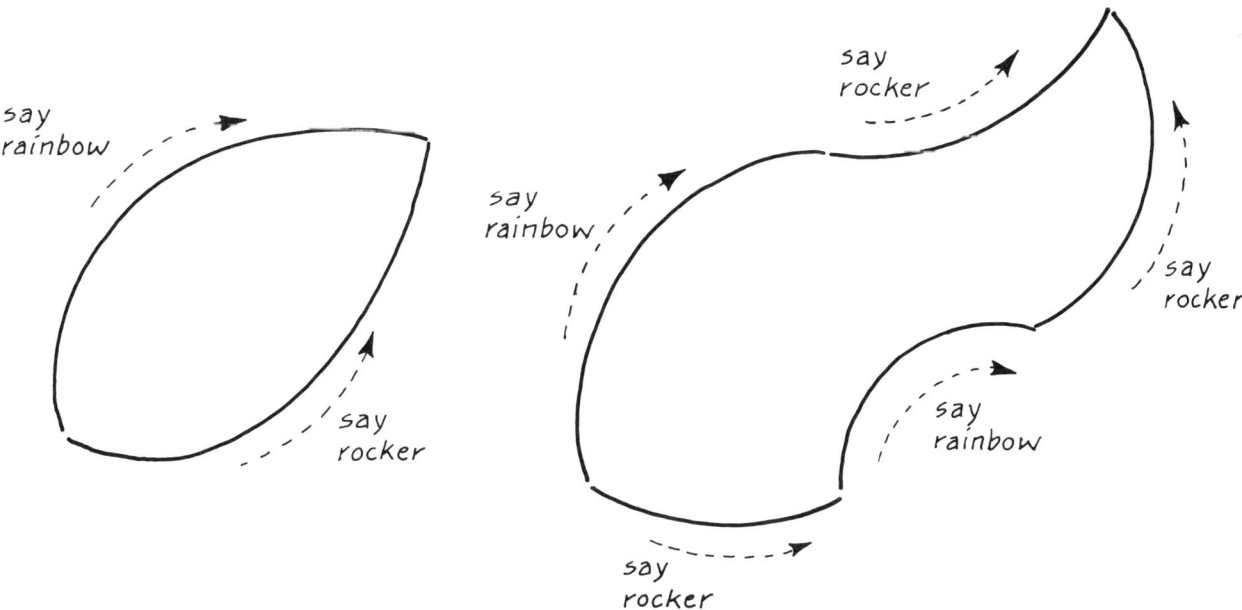

25

# Procedures

Pass out blue construction paper, scissors, crayons, and paste. Let the students choose another piece of colored construction paper for their flowers and a half sheet of green construction paper for the leaves and stems. (For very young children, you may wish to cut the stems with a paper cutter and have them ready.)

**STEP**

Tell the students they will now draw their flowers. Have them lay their hands on their papers and draw around them. Their fingers should be tightly together, with thumbs folded in on their palms. (They will not be tracing around the thumb.) Tell them to close up their shapes at the bottoms so that they resemble flowers.

**STEP**

Tell the students to cut out their flowers and paste them to the blue paper.

**STEP**

Review with the students how to draw the leaves. Direct them to draw, cut out, and paste the stem and leaves to their pictures.

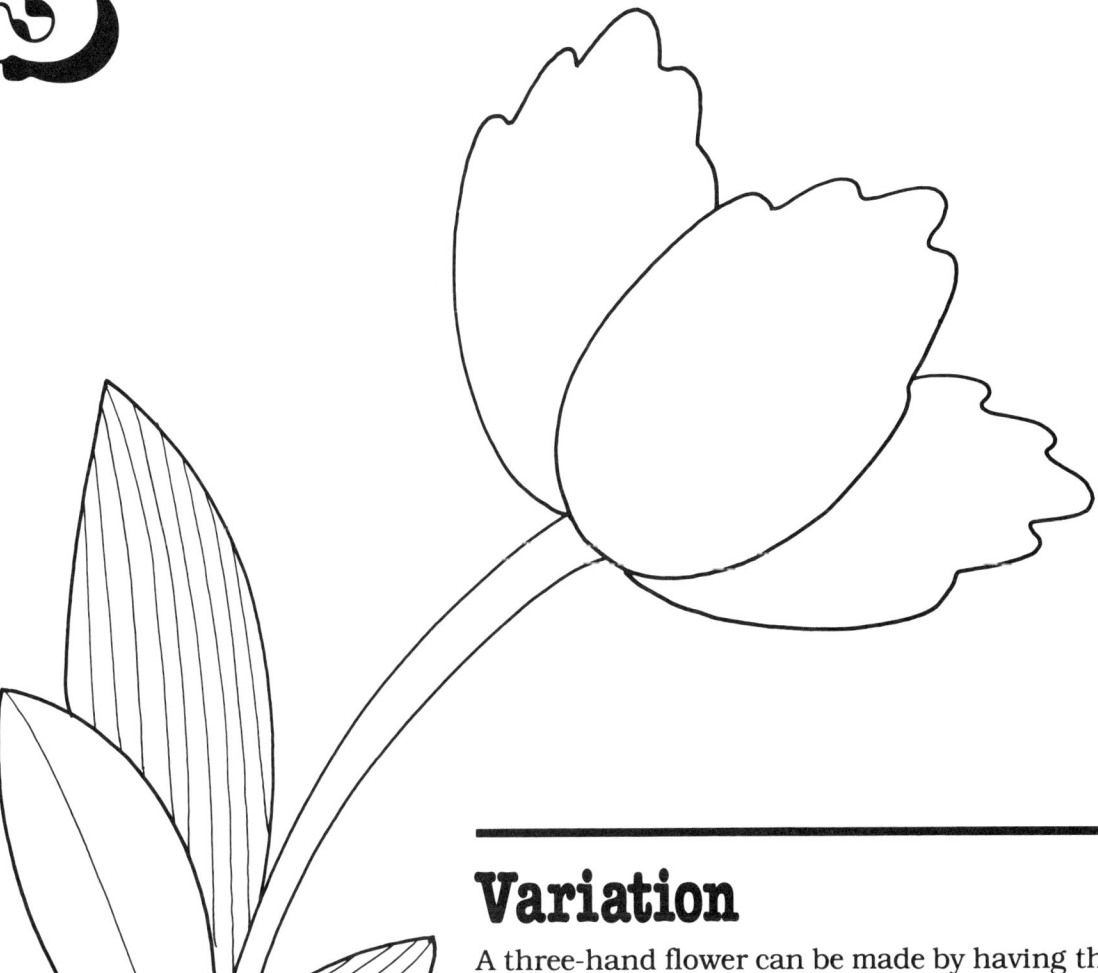

## Variation

A three-hand flower can be made by having the students draw around their hands three times and cut out the three shapes. These are then pasted to each other by pasting the two side parts to the back of the center one, as shown. Tell the students to paste their flower parts together first, and then paste the stem underneath.

# Rabbit Puppets

**Objective:** Using a paper-folding procedure, students will create rabbit puppets. This activity may be adapted to make people, cats, dogs, and the like.

## Materials

9" × 12" white construction paper

scissors

crayons

paste

## Procedures

Pass out paper, crayons, scissors, and paste to the students. Tell them they are going to make rabbit puppets, and they must listen carefully to your directions. Demonstrate each step for the students, then repeat the step along with them. Check on their progress continually, so no one is frustrated.

### STEP 1

Have the children place their papers horizontally on their desks. Walk around the room measuring three inches down from the top of each paper and placing a dot at that point. Explain, "We are going to fold our papers in thirds, long edges together." Place your paper on the chalkboard and demonstrate this step. "First, fold the bottom of the paper up to the dot. Be sure the side edges of the paper meet exactly. Then press hard on the crease. Now fold the creased edge up to the top edge of the paper. Be sure the edges are straight across the top. Press hard along the fold to make another crease."

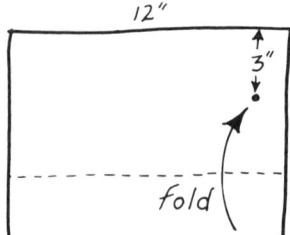

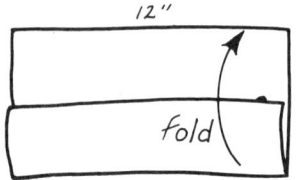

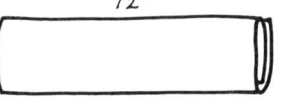

Walk around the room and check to be sure that the students have been successful with Step 1 and that the folded papers are lying flat on their desks as shown.

## STEP

"Now we're going to fold the paper in half from left to right, bringing the short edges together. Fold A to B. Press hard on the fold."

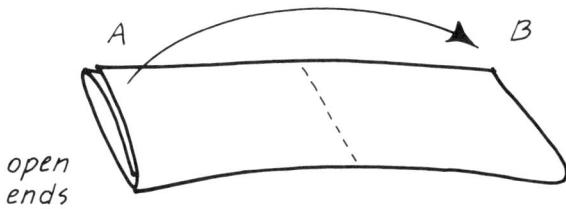

## STEP

Demonstrate the next fold for the students as shown here. Do it again with them, then walk around the room assisting those who need help. "Fold the right edge of top layer A to the left, back to C. Fold the bottom layer B back to C and crease crisply. You will see that we have created finger pockets in the back to operate our puppets." Insert your fingers in the pockets and demonstrate to the students how the puppet works. Then help those who need assistance.

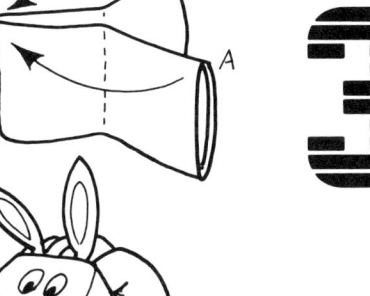

## STEP

Provide the students with pieces of white, pink, and black construction paper. Discuss with the students the features they might wish to add to their rabbits—ears, eyes, nose, whiskers. Suggest using the rainbow and rocker method for drawing the ears. (See page 25.) When drawing the ears add a tab at one end. Paste this tab inside the edge of the top pocket. The ears then fold toward the face so they will stand up. Encourage the students to make big eyes and thin whiskers.

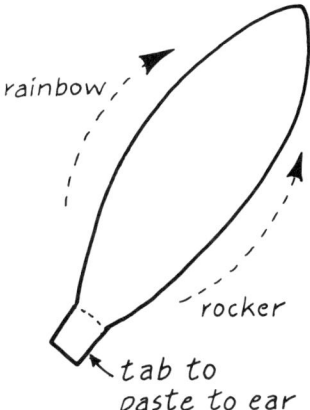

# Mosaic Designs

## Objective:
The students will create free-form mosaic designs.

## Materials

colored construction paper (a good opportunity to use your scraps)

9" × 12" manila paper

crayons

scissors

paste

## Demonstration/Motivation

You may wish to show some examples of mosaics in various art forms. This activity can be coordinated with a study of Roman history. On the chalkboard, show the students how to draw a free-form design. Tell them they will fill in each area of their designs with small pieces of colored paper. Each area will be a different color. They may use colors more than once, but caution the students not to have two areas of the same color touching each other.

## Procedures

Pass out paper, crayons, scissors, and paste.

### STEP

Tell the students to draw their designs on the manila paper with crayon.

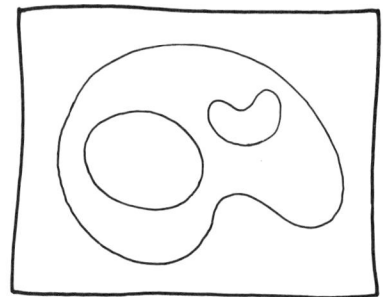

**STEP**

Place separate piles of small pieces of colored paper on a table, each pile a different color. Have each student choose a color and take one handful of paper in that color.

**STEP**

Have each student spread a thin layer of paste in one area of the design and then press the small pieces of colored paper onto it in straight lines or curves. If they need to, the students can trim the pieces to fit. Continue this process until the first area is completely covered.

**STEP**

Tell the students to take back to the table any leftover pieces of paper and choose another color. Have them repeat the pasting process until the design is completely filled in. Remind the students not to have the same color in two areas that are touching each other. As you go around the classroom, hold up well-done mosaic designs as examples for others to follow.

# Variation

Instead of free-form designs, the students may fill in simple drawings such as figures, animals, or insects. Postage stamps can be substituted for colored paper, if you have access to an ample supply.

# Fish 'n' Fun

**Objective:** Using a cutting and pasting procedure, students will create aquarium scenes.

## Materials

colored construction paper cut into small pieces

12" × 18" light blue construction paper

crayons

paste

## Demonstration/Motivation

Discuss aquariums with the students. Elicit from them the definition of aquarium: a glass tank in which fish (or other water animals) and plants live. Some animals they might mention are snails, goldfish, guppies, turtles, salamanders, tadpoles, and sea horses. Discuss reasons for having plants in an aquarium—they provide oxygen and hiding places for the fish.

## Procedures

Pass out a piece of light blue paper, paste, and crayons to each student. Draw a facsimile of the art paper on the chalkboard and show the students how to draw a fish shape. Make the fish fairly large.

32

**STEP**

Tell the students this is only one way to draw a fish, and, if they know a better way, that would be fine. Tell the students to draw a fish in their aquariums like the example on the chalkboard. Walk around the room to be sure all students understand your instructions.

**STEP**

Pass out small pieces of construction paper and paste. Have each student spread a thin layer of paste in one area of the fish and then press the small pieces of paper onto it. Tell them they will repeat this process until the fish are completely filled in. It's alright if the pieces overlap or lie on top of each other. The fish may be all one color, two colors, or a combination of many colors. Tell the students to draw and cut out an eye and paste it on the fish, too.

**STEP**

When the students are finished, tell them to draw and color some plants in their aquariums. Remind them that their fish need to breathe and hide.

# Spring-a-lings

**Objective:** Using a paper-folding and cutting technique, students will make spring-a-lings.

## Materials

colored 12" × 18" construction paper or colored bond paper (this is easier for students to cut)

scissors

yarn or thread

## Procedures

Pass out paper and scissors. Tell the students they are going to make "spring-a-lings." They must listen to your directions carefully and watch as you demonstrate each step.

### STEP 1

"First we are going to make a square. Put your piece of paper on your desk, with a short side facing you. Fold the right bottom corner over to the left, until the edges meet. Press down hard along the fold to crease it well. Carefully cut off the excess piece at the top and discard it."

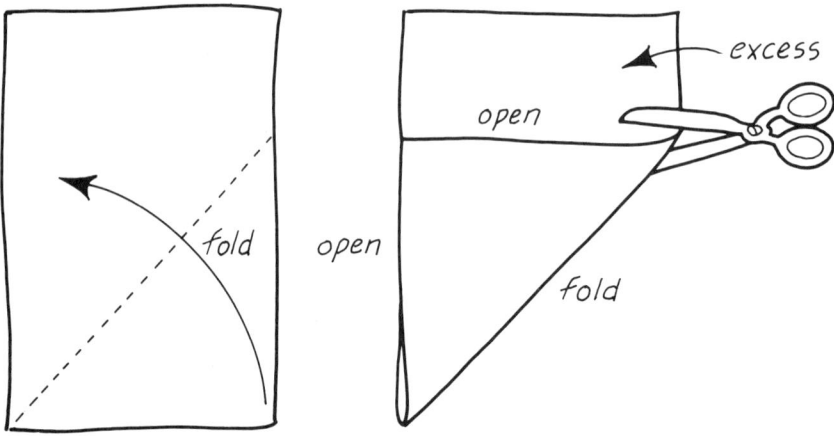

**STEP**

"The folded paper you have left is a triangle. Place it on your desk with the point facing toward you. Fold it in half from right to left, two times, each fold creating another triangle." Demonstrate this to the students.

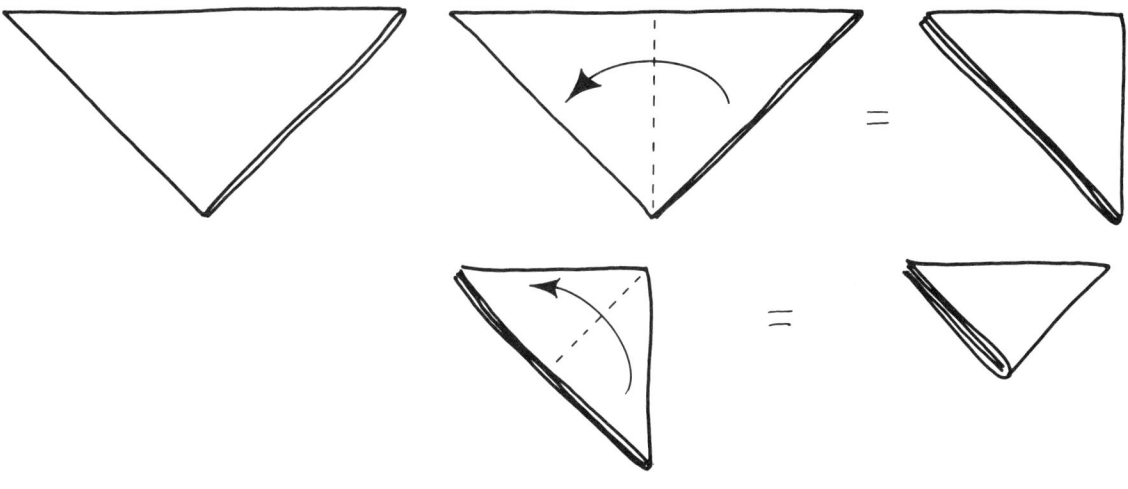

**STEP**

Have the students place their papers on their desks with the closed fold toward them and the open sides of the triangle facing left and right. Check to be sure all students have their triangles in this position.

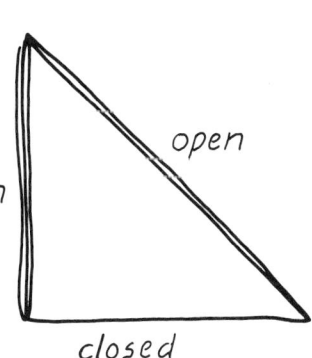

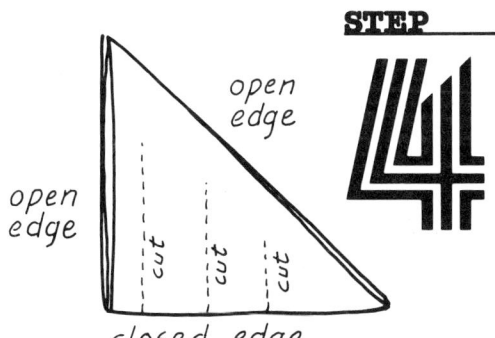

**STEP**

Demonstrate to the students how to make three cuts from the closed edge of the triangle almost to the edge of the slanted open edge. While students are doing this step, walk around the room and help those who need it.

**STEP**

"Now turn your triangle to the open edge you almost cut through and make three cuts from the open edge almost to the closed edge." Demonstrate these steps, then help those who need it.

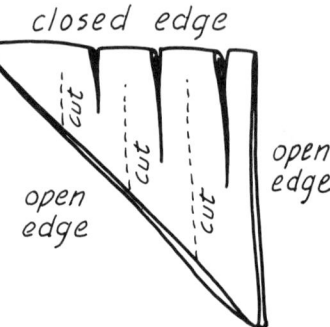

**STEP**

"Gently open up the triangles, one by one, until you have a flat, square shape again. Do this very carefully so you don't tear the paper." Demonstrate as you talk.

**STEP**

Pass by each student's desk, and using a toothpick or pencil, poke a tiny hole in the very center of the spring-a-ling. Make a knot at one end of the yarn or thread and insert the other end into the hole. Then show the students how to carefully hold the thread and gently pull down on each side of the spring-a-ling to extend it.

# Variation

At Christmas, the students can put paste and glitter on the paper after it is folded. The extended spring-a-ling then becomes a decorative Christmas tree that can be hung from the ceiling.

# III The Basics Plus One or Two

# Teddy Bears on Parade

**Objective:** Students will draw teddy bears and texture them with coffee grounds.

## Materials

9" × 12" manila paper

crayons

small pieces of black construction paper

paste (diluted to a thin consistency)

medium-size, flat-head paintbrushes

newspapers

used coffee grounds (thoroughly dried)

can of hair spray

## Demonstration/Motivation

The day before you plan to begin this activity, ask the students to bring their teddy bears to school. Display them in the room for fun and inspiration. Comment about these wonderful bears and let the students tell about them.

## Procedures

Pass out manila paper and crayons. Tell the students they are going to draw teddy bears.

**STEP 1**

Have each student lightly sketch a large bear sitting down. Tell the students the sketch lines won't show later, so they need not worry if the arms and legs overlap the body. Tell them to draw the ears, arms, and legs, but not the eyes, nose, and mouth. They will cut these features from construction paper. Advise the students not to color in the bear—only an outline of the body is needed. Draw a bear on the chalkboard to serve as a model.

**STEP**

After the bears are drawn, have each student get small pieces of black construction paper and cut out two eyes, a nose, and a mouth. Before the students paste on the eyes, have them draw two circles (larger than the cutout eyes) on the face where the eyes will go. (These areas will not be covered by the coffee grounds.) Now have the students paste the eyes (in the center of the circles), nose, and mouth on the bears.

*leave uncovered (no coffee grounds)*

*black eye pasted on*

**STEP**

Call groups of five students each to the table and show them how to put on the bear's "fur." (Provide an activity for those who finish their drawings and are waiting their turns at the table.)

**STEP**

Tell the students to spread the paste mixture on the bodies of their bears with the paintbrushes. Then have the students generously sprinkle the coffee grounds on the bodies. When the bodies are completely filled in, tell each student to spread the paste on the head, ears, arms, and legs and fill them in with the coffee grounds. Caution the students not to spread the paste mixture on the eyes, nose, mouth, or pads of the feet. These areas will remain clear.

**STEP**

Shake off the excess coffee grounds and place the teddy bears on newspapers to dry.

## STEP 6

The next day, or when the paste is dry, spray the bears with the hair spray for protection. The bears are ready to parade on the walls of your room or hall.

# Tree Seasons

**Objective:** Students will illustrate the four seasons of the year with tissue-paper trees.

## Materials

9" × 12" blue construction paper

crayons

paste

small pieces of tissue paper (pink, white, red, orange, yellow, and green)

## Demonstration/Motivation

Discuss the four seasons of the year. Have the students look out the classroom windows and describe the trees they see. What season of the year is it? Do the trees indicate the season? How do the trees look during the other three seasons?

## Procedures

Pass out the blue construction paper and crayons. Tell the students they are going to draw trees that represent the four seasons of the year.

**STEP**

Show the students how to fold their papers into fourths. (Fold in half and then in half again.) Tell them to open their papers now and lay them flat on their desks.

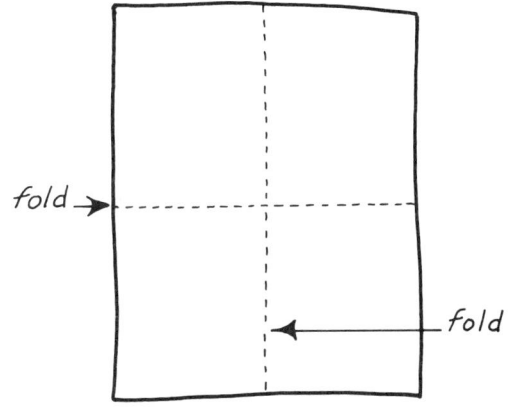

**STEP**

Tape your opened paper to the chalkboard, so the shorter edge is parallel to the chalkboard tray. "In the first frame of your paper, use a brown crayon and sketch the trunk and branches of a tree." Demonstrate this on the paper attached to the chalkboard. "Now, let's make this a blossoming tree as we would see in the spring. What color should the blossoms be?" Lead the students to respond with pink and white. "I will give you each a handful of pink and white tissue-paper pieces. Take a piece and crunch it up. Put a tiny bit of paste on a tree branch and lay the tissue on it." Show the students what you mean. "Do the same with each tiny piece, until your tree is covered. Your tree may have all pink blossoms, all white, or a mixture of both."

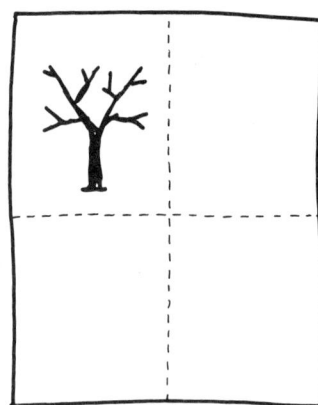

**STEP**

When most of the students are finished with the spring tree, discuss the next season—summer. "Which season will be next in your picture? Summer is correct. How would a tree look in summer? Would it be all green? Here is some green tissue for you. Paste it on the same way you did the pink and white tissue. Cover the whole tree."

**STEP**

Discuss the next two frames with the students. The fall season picture will use red, brown, orange, and yellow tissue paper. Elicit from the students the observation that the winter tree will be bare. The leaves are gone. Only the trunk and branches will be in the picture.

# Christmas Wreaths

**Objective:** Using a cutting and pasting technique, students will make decorative Christmas wreaths.

## Materials

red and green construction paper

rimmed paper plates (one for each student)

scissors

crayons

paste

hole punch

## Procedures

Using a hole punch, cut out eight red holly berries for each student. (Put aside until later.) Pass out paper plates and scissors.

### STEP

Tell each student to cut out the inside of the paper plate along the rim line. To get started, punch a hole in the center with scissors and then cut over to the rim line. Caution the students not to cut through the rim. Demonstrate, and assist as needed.

**STEP**

Pass out the green construction paper and crayons. Show the students how to draw and cut holly leaves. Suggest they use the "rainbow" and "rocker" method. (See page 25.)

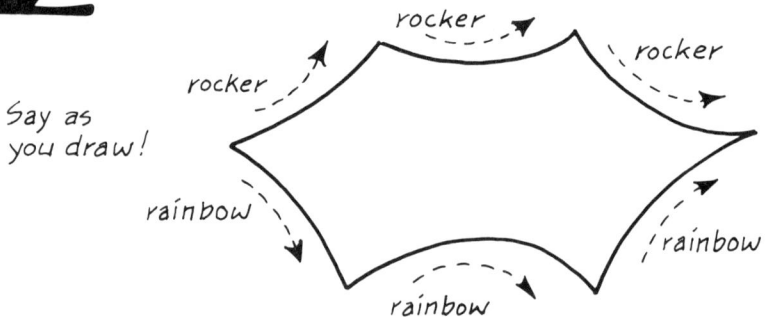

For younger students, you may wish to provide holly leaf patterns. Tell the students to draw and cut out twenty leaves—enough to completely cover their paper plates.

**STEP**

When the students are finished cutting out their leaves, demonstrate how to paste them on the paper plates. Tell them to overlap the leaves, so no part of the paper plate will show. As they are pasting, walk around the room and show examples of good work.

**STEP**

Pass out eight holly berries to each student. Tell the students to paste them randomly around the wreath. Have them look at the sample wreath if they need help with the placement of their berries.

## Variation

Use green foil wrapping paper for the holly leaves. Ask each student to bring a small red bow from home, or provide fluffy yarn for the students to tie into bows. Attach these bows to the wreaths.

# Autograph Mirrors

**Objective:** Using their own signatures, the students will create autograph mirrors.

## Materials

12" × 18" colored construction paper

white ditto paper

scissors

crayons

glue

mirror (optional)

## Demonstration/Motivation

Have a discussion about what an autograph is. Ask if students have ever signed their autographs and exchanged them with others. Have they ever asked for the autograph of a famous person? Do they have autograph books?

## Procedures

Tell the students they are going to collect some autographs from their classmates. They will make autograph mirrors and exchange them with one another. Pass out crayons, scissors, and a sheet of ditto paper to each student.

**STEP**

"Place the ditto paper flat on your desk, so that the short end is toward you. Fold up the short end just a little way, about one quarter of the page." Demonstrate with a piece of paper on the chalkboard.

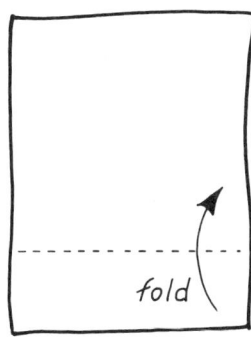

**STEP**

"Unfold the paper so that it is flat on your desk again. Write your first name in cursive on the fold line, using any color crayon you choose. Press heavily with your crayon. You will probably need to go over your signature twice to make it very dark." Using the chalkboard again, demonstrate how to autograph the paper with crayon.

**STEP**

"Now fold the paper together again, along the same fold line as before. Rub hard in one direction using the side of your pencil. Exert as much pressure as possible. Unfold the paper. Your name should have rubbed off on the other side of the fold. If it hasn't, try making your name darker or pressing down harder as you rub." Demonstrate the one-way rubbing stroke by placing your folded paper on the chalkboard.

**STEP**

"Now everyone is ready to cut out an autograph mirror. Do it this way." Demonstrate while explaining, "Cut around the broad outline of your signature. You do not need to cut out each letter exactly. Cut around both your autograph and its mirror image."

**STEP**

Pass out paste. "Now I'm going to give everyone a number." Number off half the class, then give the same numbers to the other half. If the number of students is not even, you will need to give yourself a number and do your name also. "Find the person who has the same number as you and exchange autographs with that person. Then paste just the bottom half of the cutout autograph on the colored paper. The other half will stand up." Demonstrate this step for the students.

**STEP**

When all students have exchanged and pasted the autographs on their papers, have them do another autograph and exchange again. This time pair the numbers differently (1–14, 2–13, 3–12, and so on). More autographs can be made and exchanged as time permits. It is also fun to let the students look at their autographs in a mirror.

# Variation

Students can color their autographs before cutting out and exchanging them. They then become autograph designs.

# Magnetic Magic

**Objective:** Students will make pictures with movable parts.

## Materials

9″ × 12″ manila paper

tagboard or cardboard cut into 9″ × 1″ strips (one for each student)

magnetic tape cut into 1″ × ½″ and ½″ × ¾″ pieces (one each for each student)

crayons

scissors

## Procedures

Pass out manila paper, crayons, and scissors. Tell the students they are going to draw pictures with movable parts. The movable parts can be anything they want them to be: people, animals, cars.

**STEP**

Draw a facsimile of the art paper on the chalkboard. Tell the students you want a kite as the movable part of your picture. Ask them to suggest a background for the kite. Then cut out a kite from construction paper and place it on the chalkboard picture. Discuss the correct size for it with the students. Lead them to realize that the movable object must be in correct proportion to the rest of the picture.

**STEP**

Tell the students to draw simple scenes on their papers.

**STEP**

Give the students small pieces of colored construction paper and tell them to draw and cut out their movable objects.

**STEP**

Call the students to your desk, one at a time or in small groups, as they finish their backgrounds. Help the students to attach the magnetic tape, first to their cutout objects, then to the 9″ × 1″ cardboard strips. (The larger piece of tape goes on the cardboard strip, the smaller piece on the movable object.)

**STEP**

Show the students how to make their objects move. Put the movable object in place on the picture and the cardboard strip behind the picture. As you move the strip back and forth across the back of the picture, the object on the front of the paper will move.

# Sun Catchers

**Objective:** Students will create transparent designs to hang in the windows.

## Materials

- wax paper (an 8" piece for each student)
- colored tissue paper
- black yarn cut into 20–24" lengths
- glue diluted with water to half strength
- small paintbrushes
- small containers for glue mixture
- scissors

## Procedures

Cut the tissue paper into postage-stamp-size pieces. You will be demonstrating and working with one small group at a time, so provide each student with a piece of manila paper for free art while you work with the others. If possible, make a "sun catcher" ahead of time to show the class. Pass out wax paper, yarn, glue mixture, and paintbrushes. Tell the students they are going to make sun catchers.

### STEP 1

Tell the students to place the wax paper flat on their desks. Have them lay the lengths of yarn on the wax paper, creating a free-form design. Demonstrate this step and help those who need it.

### STEP 2

Have the students lift the yarn carefully in one area, put a little of the glue mixture on the wax paper, and secure the yarn to it. Tell them to work a small area at a time until all the yarn is pasted in place.

**STEP**

Show the students how to "paint" a small area inside the yarn design with the brush and glue mixture. Then take a handful of colored tissue pieces and smooth them, one at a time, on that area. Stress that the pieces will overlap so every bit of the wax paper is covered. Tell the students to "paint" another area and repeat the process until the whole design is covered with the tissue. Suggest that they glue only one small area at a time as the glue tends to dry quickly. Check their progress to be sure that the tissue pieces are glued securely.

**STEP**

Lightly "paint" the surface of the design with the glue mixture when finished. It will secure the tissue while drying clear.

**STEP**

Lay the sun catchers on a flat surface to dry overnight. The next day, cut off the excess wax paper just outside the yarn line and tape the sun catchers on the windows.

# Variation

The gluing process may be repeated on the other side of the wax paper, so there is no right or wrong side to it.

# Ghosts!

**Objective:** Using facial-tissue ghosts as the focal point, students will create Halloween scenes.

## Materials

- box of white facial tissues
- 9" × 12" black construction paper
- yarn or thread
- black marker
- paste
- crayons

## Procedures

Pass out paper, two tissues, paste, length of yarn or thread, and crayons to each student. Tell them they are going to make Halloween night pictures. Each picture will have a white ghost made of facial tissue.

**STEP 1**

To make the ghosts, roll one of the tissues into a ball. Put the other tissue over this "head." Tie the yarn or thread around the ghost's neck. Demonstrate these steps to the students. Then walk around the room and assist where needed.

**STEP 2**

Show the students how to make two big eyes on the ghost's face with a black marker. Then pass the marker around for the students to use.

**STEP 3**

Pass out the black paper while discussing what might be seen on Halloween night. Tell the students to paste their ghosts on the paper and then draw in the rest of the Halloween night scene with their crayons. Remind them to color firmly and heavily so that the colors will stand out.

# Leaf Rubbings

**Objective:** Students will develop an appreciation for art in nature by making textured leaf rubbings.

## Materials

12" × 18" manila paper

crayons

green leaves

## Demonstration/Motivation

Ask the students to bring three or four green leaves to school, or take a walk with the students around the school grounds and collect leaves for this activity. You can coordinate this activity with a science lesson by helping the students identify the types of leaves they find.

## Procedures

Pass out paper and crayons. Tell the students they are going to make leaf rubbings. Demonstrate how to make a leaf rubbing by laying the paper over the leaf and rubbing lightly but evenly over the surface with the side of a crayon. Warn the students not to let the paper move while the rubbing is in process. Rub back and forth across the leaf until the veins and contours have etched themselves onto the paper. Let the students begin their rubbings as you walk around the room assisting where needed. When they are finished with their own leaves, let the students exchange leaves with other students and repeat the process until their papers are full. The more advanced students might like to write the identity of the leaves on their papers.

## Variation

Use a variety of textured flat objects to make rubbings: scissors, paper clips, nail file, keys, coins, pieces of wood, or ruler. Ask students to bring objects from home and let them trade and share.